THE UNFILLABLE SHOES

RINA GAUDIOSI CIGNARELLA

First edition 2019
Copyright © Rina Gaudiosi Cignarella: rinacig@bigpond.com
Artwork by The Illustrators: www.theillustrators.com.au
Title: The Unfillable Shoes

THE UNFILLABLE
SHOES

This is a true story of Joseph who left his home and family to come to Australia for a better life.

He worked hard and became rich enough to go back home and build homes for all of his family. He became the landowner. He never forgot his poor beginnings and his family's struggles. He always remembered the kindness of a stranger giving him the unfillable shoes.

My name is

....

My name is Joseph. I am a businessman who after many years of hard work and sacrifices, have successfully created my own construction business.

On a very cold winter's day I was on my way to a business meeting in the city dressed accordingly, fine suit and the most comfortable pair of shoes. I noticed a little boy walking bare-foot in a back street of the poorer part of the city.

This child was barely clothed; my heart broke for him. He would be perhaps eight or nine years old. The poverty was overwhelming.

Dedicated to

León D., Atabey, Kian Milo and
Adrián Emilio for all I learn from
you. To Roberto for the long
conversations that eventually
become stories.

A special thanks to Ismalia
Gutiérrez, Gloria Prósper, Edna
Román and Joanie Mencher Carlise
for being so generous with their
time and criticism.

This is the story of Tulipán, the Puerto Rican giraffe.

Tulipán was a happy giraffe who went to school every day and always did her very best.

She often sat in the front row to keep from being distracted and thereby give her full attention to the teacher.

At other times, if a classmate complained about her long neck, the teacher would ask her to sit in the back.

Sitting in the last seat of a row also had its charm. From there, she could see everyone.

A lot went on in her
classroom that could only be
appreciated from the back of the
room. Some students passed notes
to each other, others whispered
to their neighbor, some would
throw things, and others would
even chew gum. It was very easy
to be distracted back there.

That's why she preferred
to sit up front.

She loved it when the teacher sat the class in a circle or at a big table. This way she could clearly see and hear the teacher, and also see and interact with her classmates.

Do you know the one thing
Tulipán did not like about school?

She didn't like exams!

Surprisingly, although Tulipán participated in class, asked questions and studied hard, she didn't get **As** on her exams.

For example, one time she was asked on an exam: "Who discovered Puerto Rico?"
Immediately she thought of Christopher Columbus, but his name was not among the options.

Who discovered Puerto Rico?

a. the Taínos
b. the Italians
c. the Spanish
d. none of the above

She didn't choose **d** only because she saw some truth in the other answers.

She knew the Taínos were the first inhabitants of Puerto Rico, that the Spanish financed the expedition and that Columbus was Italian. Any one of these could be right, so she ignored **d**.

She scratched her head as she tried to figure this puzzle out and thought, "which is the best answer?"

She decided to pick "the Taínos" because they were in Puerto Rico first, so, they must have discovered the island. Columbus had just bumped into the island on his way somewhere else. That is why she answered **a**.

When she got her exam back, Tulipán saw that the expected answer was **d**. She was frustrated that she knew so much about how Borinquen became Puerto Rico, but had no way to show it.

"Why couldn't a question have more than one answer?" she asked herself.

"Why is there only one way to think?" she pondered.

"How come the story of Columbus was better known than the story of the Taínos?"

"Why isn't learning to question as important as learning to answer?

"What is school for, to educate, to confuse, to explore, to limit, to do **what,** exactly?"

Another time, there was a fill-in-the-blank exercise:

When you knock on a door and someone asks from inside, "Who is it?", you should answer, "It is _____."

   a. You
   b. I
   c. him
   d. me

"That's easy," thought Tulipán as she chose **d**.

She was quite surprised when she found out the required answer was **b**. "Who says, it is I?" Tulipán asked herself, perplexed.

When she arrived home, her Mom explained that "me" was not incorrect, just informal. Most people say " It's me." Tulipán smiled, feeling much better.

Another thing Tulipán did not like was the day the corrected exams were returned to the students; it was a sad day for many.

The adults waiting at the school gate to pick up their children at the end of the day were always comparing grades. Tulipán disliked this competition and asked her mother to wait for her away from the crowd.

Her mother did so.

Nobody questioned the grades.

Nobody asked why a different answer was chosen.

"Couldn't another answer be correct in somebody else's mind?" Tulipán wondered.

"Things are just not that simple," her mind told her.

Tulipán thought, and thought and thought about this for a very long time.

"Can a grade on an exam REALLY measure what you know?"

She asked herself this question over and over again. Her mind and heart told her that she knew much more than what her grades revealed.

She knew she could think; she thought all the time. Her mind was constantly at work as she listened to what her ears heard, she observed what her eyes saw, she smelled what her nose sniffed, she savored what her tongue tasted, and she felt what her skin touched in the world around her.

She learned so much through her five senses, things not necessarily taught in school, things not mentioned on any exam.

She helped her mother fix the car, cooked with her father, took care of her little brother, invented games with her friends, treated everyone with respect and kindness, read books, drew pictures, and much, much more.

Yet she couldn't help asking herself, "How do you know that you know?"

Until one day, building sand castles on the beach, Tulipán noticed a space between the waves. Her grandmother had taught her that this was the sign of a riptide.

She alerted the swimmers to the danger, but few would listen to such a young giraffe.

A teenager jumped into the water anyway. The riptide grabbed him and began pulling him out to sea.

"Swim parallel to the shore," Tulipán shouted. All of a sudden, everyone began repeating her instructions, "Swim parallel to the shore," they yelled and pointed.

The teenager understood, followed the instructions and was saved.

"That is to know," concluded Tulipán.

After that frightful day, Tulipán was not so focused on getting **As**; now she concentrated on using everything she knew to help herself and others.

One day, she got an **A** on an exam and the teacher said, "Congratulations, Tuli, you did it!"

Tulipán just smiled and said, "Chévere," although she knew that was not so important.

And she lived happily ever after.

Made in the USA
Middletown, DE
12 August 2016